Museum Publications

Lace-Making in Hamilton by Jessie Lochhead M.A.

Hand-Loom Weaving in Hamilton and District by G. Walker

Hamilton Palace, a photographic record by G. Walker

Transport and farm equipment in Hamilton District Museum by G. Walker

Published by Hamilton District Libraries and Museum dept.
Chief Librarian C. Smith, A.L.A.

Illus. 1 Breaking his fast   photo by A.H. Allan

Victorian and Edwardian photographs

from the photographic collection of
Hamilton District Libraries and Museum,
as displayed in the Museum

Compiled and introduced by G. Walker

Edited by C. Smith A.L.A., Chief Librarian

Layout by G. Walker

Introduction

In addition to early professional firms like that of T. & R. Annan, Hamilton had some gifted amateur photographers in the latter part of the nineteenth century. These men faithfully recorded the town and the surrounding countryside and we are fortunate indeed that so many of their slides and negatives survived and were deposited in the Library. The late Mr. Wm. Stewart, librarian at Hamilton from 1940-73, realised the value of these photographs as a historical record and started to index the material which had been left to him by his predecessor Mr. A. Brown. Mr. Stewart also had the streets of the town photographed before re-development and tried to increase the stock of old scenes.

We have continued collecting over the years and though the additions generally come singly as old faded and yellow prints, which have to be re-photographed, we have on occasion been more fortunate. One such was the donation from Mr. Henry Allan of Edinburgh of several hundred glass negatives which had been produced or collected by his father Mr. A.H. Allan. Mr. Allan senr., who was born and educated in Hamilton, was an outstanding photographer and his negatives date from c.1860 to the first World War. They include scenes of farming, fishing, people at work, Lanarkshire views and character studies. We have reproduced several of Mr. Allan's photographs here, but as we are unable to identify the other individual photographers who have contributed, we have omitted names except on the frontispiece.

Though we cannot acknowledge them by name, we can pay tribute to the quality of their work. When we consider the slow emulsions they worked with, the slow shutter speeds of their stand cameras and the weight of their equipment, we marvel at the results they produced. To them, the scenes they recorded were commonplace. The streets, with children playing and people walking in the road-way, were as they always had been. But for us, their work illustrates the days of our grand and great grand parents better than any written contemporary account. It is apparent too from some of the photographs that the contrast in the lifestyles of the different classes in society was even more marked in the nineteenth century than it is today.

We cannot from our stock alone and in this small book cover adequately the whole of the present Hamilton District and have not attempted to do so. However, we have tried to show as wide and as varied a selection as possible from the prints which have been and are presently on display in the Museum.

G.W.

Contents

Illus. 2 The Old Cross, Hamilton c.1880 from Cadzow Street

Illus. 3 The Sheilinghill c.1890

Illus. 4 A Hawker with his barrow in Campbell Street outside Stirling's Coach Factory, c.1880

Illus. 5 Fishwives and their husbands confer in Portland Place, c.1880

Illus. 6 (left) Collecting water at the pump in Muir Street c.1880. In the 17th. century, Muir Street or Wynd was the road to the common muir (Almada Street area). The buildings shown date from this period.

Illus. 8 (overleaf) A lady with a perambulator crosses in front of a horse bus and an oncoming coach in Townhead Street c.1880

Illus. 7 (above) A parish pump discussion at Meikle Earnock c.1890.

Illus. 9 A railway lorry comes up the Postgate c.1900.

Illus. 10 Harvesters with a harvest cart on the Glebe Farm near Park Road c.1890. Up to the first World War, the countryside was within easy walking distance of most town dwellers.

Illus. 11 Harvesting by the Mission Hall in Lowwaters Road c.1880

Illus. 12 (left) Before the evening milking near Quarter c. 1900

Illus. 13 (above) Cutting barley near Stonehouse c.1890.

Illus. 14 (overleaf) The stackyard

Illus. 15 Sowing and Harrowing in the spring of 1900.

19

Illus. 16 The Linthaugh and the river Avon, Stonehouse, c.1900.

Illus. 17 Lawrie Street and Argyle Street, Stonehouse from the Railway Bridge, c.1890.

Illus. 18 (above) Raploch Street, Larkhall, c.1890.

Illus. 19 (above) The Cross, Larkhall, c.1890.

Illus. 20 (right) Millheugh village from the river, c.1890.

22

Illus. 21 The Pirn wheel. Margaret Semple "winnin' the pirns" (winding silk onto bobbins) for her father's weaving loom.

Illus. 22 Pram wheels, three boys and a hill.

Illus. 23 Going in—School lines at Quarter School, c.1900.

Illus. 24 Coming out—Children 'skailing' from Lowwaters School, c.1900.

Illus. 25 (overleaf) Learning with mother, a girl's lot was often a hard one.

Illus. 26 (above) The 1890 'bools' season in full swing in the New Wynd.

Illus. 27 (overleaf) The harshness of a tinker's life is shown in this fine shot by Mr. Allan, c.1900.

Illus. 28 The Sunday School trip of 1900, a yearly outing to a farmer's field.

Illus. 29 Officers and their ladies in Cadzow Street returning from the annual parade of the Yeomanry in the Low Parks, Hamilton, c.1890.

Illus. 31 (above) A mounted band of Yeomanry in the Low Parks. As few regiments of Yeomanry could muster a turnout like this, it is probable that the band were regulars borrowed for the parade.

Illus. 30 (left) Lanarkshire Yeomanry in Cadzow Street watched by admiring youngsters, c.1890.

Illus. 32 The Boy's Brigade parade in Quarry Street for the Coronation Parade of 1910.

Illus. 33 Frisky horses upset the parade at the Old Cross, c.1890.

Illus. 34 A party of friends around the fountain in Barncluith Gardens, c.1900.

Illus. 35 Neighbours celebrate Queen Victoria's Jubilee in Orchard Street, Hamilton.

Illus. 36 Caledonian Railway locomotive No. 88 at Hamilton West, c.1870.

Illus. 37 A Goods Train on Stonehouse Viaduct, c.1910.

Illus. 38 The River Clyde and Bothwell Castle, c.1880.

Illus. 39 Bothwell village and St. Bride's Church, c.1890.

Illus. 40 Uddingston Cross showing the Lanarkshire and Glasgow Corporation tramcars, c.1910.

Illus. 41 (above) Woodview, Main Street, Uddingston, c.1910.

Illus. 42 (below) Bellshill Road and the Old Mill Road, Uddingston, c.1910.

Illus. 43 David Livingstone's house at Blantyre, c.1910.

Illus. 44 Hunthill Road, Blantyre, c.1910.

Illus. 45 Barnhill, Blantyre, c.1910.

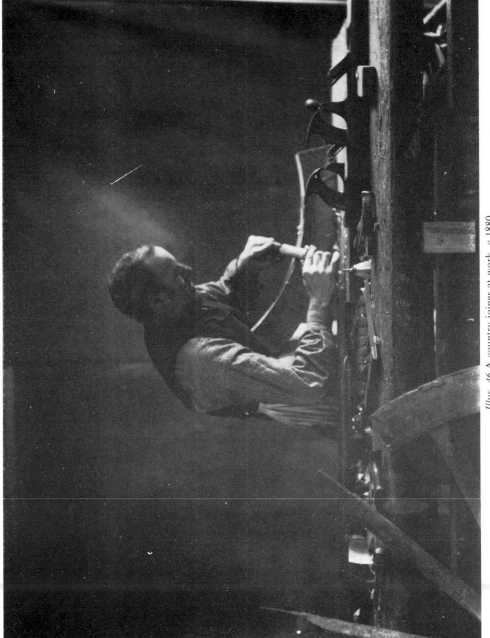

Illus. 46 A country joiner at work, c.1880.

Illus. 47 Stonehouse Quarry in the 1880s.

Illus. 48 A cobbler takes a quizzical look at a well worn boot.

Illus. 49 A girl at Hamilton Weaving Factory, c.1900.

Illus. 50 (above) Excelsior China Shop, New Cross, Hamilton, c.1880.

Illus. 51 (below) The interior of the Central Grocery shop of Larkhall Victualling Co-operative Soc. c.1910.

Illus. 52 (above) Buchanan's Library and Stationers, New Cross, Hamilton, c.1890.

Illus. 53 (below) Fresh meat on the hoof outside Nicholson's butchers shop in Lowwaters Road, c.1890.

Illus. 54 (above) A close finish on Hamilton Bowling Green, c.1870.

Illus. 55 (right) a game of 'kyles' outside the Hamilton Weaving Factory, c.1890.
'Kyles' was the name used by the old hand-loom weavers for their particular variation of the game of skittles.

Illus. 57 (above) Curling on the River Avon at Millheugh Bridge during the big freeze up of 1895.

Illus. 56 (left) Curling on Hamilton Haugh, c.1900.

Illus. 58 The 'Steamboat' at Hamilton Fair, c.1890.

Illus. 59 Roundabouts at Hamilton Fair, c.1890.